Neat, Tidy, and Clean

TEACHING SYNONYMS

BY MARY LINDEEN

The Child's World®
childsworld.com

Published by The Child's World®
1980 Lookout Drive • Mankato, MN 56003-1705
800-599-READ • www.childsworld.com

ACKNOWLEDGMENTS
The Child's World®: Mary Swensen, Publishing Director
Red Line Editorial: Editorial direction and production
The Design Lab: Design

Photographs ©: Shutterstock Images, cover (right), cover (left), 1,
5, 8, 9, 11, 13; Andrey Popov/Shutterstock Images, cover (middle);
Tracy Starr/Shutterstock Images, 2; Tristan Tan/Shutterstock
Images, 6; Erin Pence/Shutterstock Images, 10; Eric Isselee/
Shutterstock Images, 12; Kjetil Kolbjornsrud/Shutterstock Images,
14–15; Rob Holdorp/Shutterstock Images, 15

ISBN 9781503808416
LCCN 2015958424

Printed in the United States of America
Mankato, MN
June, 2016
PAO2304

ABOUT THE AUTHOR
Mary Lindeen is a writer, editor, former
elementary school teacher, and parent. She
has written more than 100 books for children.
She specializes in early literacy instruction and
creating books for young readers.

Synonyms are words that have the same or nearly the same meaning. Look for **synonyms** in this book. You will find them in **bold** type.

It is a big **job** to keep
a zoo clean.
But the zookeepers love
their **work**.

It is **hard** to organize
the orangutans.
And it is **difficult** to group
the gorillas.

The flamingoes can **wash** their own feet. The bears also **bathe** by themselves.

The tiger **likes** to use its tongue to freshen up.
And the elephant **enjoys** using its trunk.

The hippo is **happy** to get some help with its teeth.
The alligator is **glad** for help cleaning its teeth, too.

The work is done.
The zoo is **spotless**!
Everyone looks **neat**,
tidy, and **clean**.

Did you find these synonyms?

bathe/wash
clean/neat/spotless/tidy
difficult/hard
enjoys/likes
glad/happy
job/work

To Learn More

IN THE LIBRARY

Coffelt, Nancy. *Big, Bigger, Biggest!*
New York: Henry Holt, 2009.

Heinrichs, Ann. *Synonyms and Antonyms*. Mankato, MN: The Child's World, 2011.

Klayman, Neil Steven. *Boris Ate a Thesaurus*. Torrance, CA: Super Series Productions, 2011.

ON THE WEB

Visit our Web site for links about synonyms: **childsworld.com/links**

Note to Parents, Teachers, and Librarians: We routinely verify our Web links to make sure they are safe and active sites. So encourage your readers to check them out!